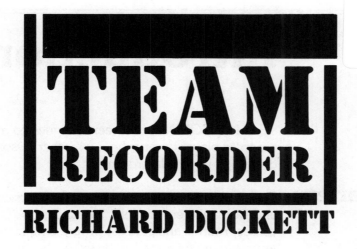

TEAM RECORDER

RICHARD DUCKETT

International Music Publications Limited

Introduction

TEAM RECORDER has been designed to meet the needs of young recorder players everywhere, whether lessons are given individually, in groups or in the classroom.

Musical variety

Each book contains a wide variety of musical styles, from the Classical and Romantic eras to folk, jazz and 'pop'. In addition there are original pieces, rounds and studies, progressing from the beginner stage to approximately Grade I standard of the *Associated Board of the Royal Schools of Music*. Furthermore, TEAM RECORDER offers material suitable for mixed ensemble as well as solos with piano accompaniment.

Ensemble pieces

The TEAM RECORDER ensemble pieces can be extended into classroom band, school orchestra or wind band. Beginners are thus offered early ensemble experience and the opportunity to share lessons with other players, whether they play treble or bass clef, C, F, B flat or E flat pitched instruments, or even guitar or keyboards. Dynamics are introduced on page 18 and are provided thereafter in all accompanied pieces.

National Curriculum

As well as offering the facility of performing, TEAM RECORDER allows young recorder players to develop listening skills, improvisation and compositional techniques consistent with the requirements of the National Curriculum. Relevant material appears throughout the book. As a guide, a well balanced group lesson of 30 minutes might consist of the following:

Lesson formats

5 mins : Listening skills (page 2 or 12)

10 mins : Reinforced learning of upper D, i.e. *Step round* (p.13) and/or *Lightly row* (p.14)

5 mins : *Play by ear* (p.15) with class split up into smaller groups if possible

5 mins : *Theory quiz*

5 mins : Ensemble pieces, e.g. *Now the day is over* (p.15)

There are many other lesson formats that can be devised by careful use of the material in TEAM RECORDER which will allow pupils to develop listening, composing and performing.

For teachers who integrate recorder work with other classroom instruments, simple percussion parts are provided for the ensemble pieces. Also included is a basic graphic display of recorder notes on the glockenspiel/chime bars.

Note:
In some of the pieces in TEAM RECORDER the key signatures appear with bracketed sharps or flats. Whereas each key signature is academically correct, the brackets serve to indicate sharps or flats that have not been introduced to the player or do not appear in the exercise or piece.

Team Recorder Ensemble

TEAM RECORDER ensemble material has been specially written so that it can be played by almost any combination of recorder, percussion, wind, brass or string players that the teacher is likely to encounter. The pieces are basically for duet, to which can be added independent (and inessential) third and fourth parts if required.

TEAM RECORDER includes ten recorder duets. Related parts for wind, brass, strings and treble recorder appear in the Supplement included with this book. It is anticipated that flute and oboe will play the recorder parts. Percussion parts and simple piano accompaniments come within the main body of the book. Appendix 1 includes a page of 'easy recorder parts' in the range of G, A and B, which allow beginners to participate with more advanced players.

This book also contains parts relating to the ensemble material in TEAM BRASS, TEAM WOODWIND and TEAM PERCUSSION. These parts are located in Appendix 2. All harmonically interlocking parts in general progress technically at the same rate, i.e. from the complete beginner stage to around Grade I.

TEAM RECORDER offers easy piano accompaniments and keyboard/guitar chords with appropriate pieces.

The ensemble material in all the TEAM books can be played by combinations of players from duet right up to full sized band or orchestra. It is up to the teacher to distribute parts in a manner which allows for a satisfactory degree of balance to be achieved.

The following symbol has been used to provide an immediate visual identification:

 A duet offering parts (in the supplement) for all wind, brass, string and percussion instruments.

Edited by BARRIE CARSON TURNER

INTERNATIONAL MUSIC PUBLICATIONS would like to thank the following publishers for permission to use arrangements of their copyright material in TEAM RECORDER.

MATCH OF THE DAY - by RHET STOLLER
© 1971 & 1992 RAK Publishing Ltd., London NW8 7BU
LOVE ME TENDER - Words and Music by VERA MATSON & ELVIS PRESLEY
© 1956 & 1992 Elvis Presley Music Inc., USA
Carlin Music Corp., London NW1 8BD
AGADOO - Words and Music by M. SYMILE, M. DELANCERY and J. PERAM
© 1985 & 1992 Editions Marouani, France
Warner Chappell Music Ltd., London WIY 3FA
DON'T SIT UNDER THE APPLE TREE (WITH ANYONE ELSE BUT ME) - Words and Music by LEW BROWN, CHARLIE TOBIAS and SAM H. STEPT
© 1942 & 1992 Robbins Music Corporation, USA
Redwood Music Ltd., London NW1 8BD/Memory Lane Music Ltd., London WC2H 8NA/EMI United Partnership Ltd., London WC2H OEA
CORONATION STREET - by ERIC SPEAR
© 1961 & 1992 Mercury Music Co. Ltd., London WC2H 0EA
HOW MUCH IS THAT DOGGIE IN THE WINDOW? - Words and Music by BOB MERRILL
© 1953 &1992 Golden Bell Songs, USA
Warner Chappell Music Ltd.,London WIY 3FA
LITTLE DONKEY - Words and Music by ERIC BOSWELL
© 1959 & 1992 Chappell Music Ltd., London W1Y 3FA
BLOWIN' IN THE WIND- Words and Music by BOB DYLAN
© 1963 & 1992 Witmark & Sons, USA
Warner Chappell Music Ltd., London WIY 3FA

Sincere thanks are extended to the following people whose criticism, advice and help in various ways has been invaluable.
MRS MOLLY WICKS, Primary school recorder co-ordinator
MRS ATHENA YARDLEY and the children of Lakey Lane School, Birmingham

First Published 1992

Cover Conception and Realisation: Ian Elwick/David Croft
Cover Photography: Andrew Southorn
Production: Stephen Clark/David Croft
Reprographics: Cloverleaf Group
Music Setting: Gillian Gower/Christine Mitchell
Instruments photographed by courtesy of Walthamstow Music Shop, London.
Typeset by: Headline Publicity Ltd.
Printed in England

TEAM RECORDER
Book only: Order ref.18112:   ISBN 1-84328-546-0.
Book & CD: Order ref. 6773A: ISBN 1-84328-668-8.

Getting started

Hold the recorder with your left hand at the top and the right hand at the bottom. Your left hand thumb covers the hole at the back and your right hand thumb holds the lower part of the instrument. The tip of the mouthpiece should be placed gently between the lips but should not touch the teeth. You must sit (or stand) up quite straight, but relaxed, holding your head and recorder up.

Use the soft pads of your fingers to cover the holes rather than your finger tips. Make sure you always cover the holes completely so that notes do not 'squeak'. When your fingers are not being used, try to keep them close to the holes so that you don't have to move them far when they are needed.

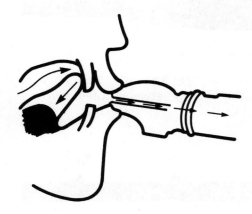

To make a sound on the recorder, take a full, relaxed breath; put your tongue behind your top teeth and then pull it away quickly as if saying the word 'do' or 'too'. This releases the air sharply into the recorder. Never blow hard into it otherwise you will overblow and 'squeak'. Always *breathe* into it.

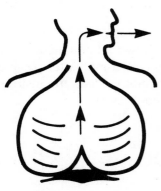

Tummy muscle

Once you can make a small sound, try to make it longer, fuller and firmer, by keeping the air stream steady. Keep your lungs quite full of air and gently pull up your tummy muscle (diaphragm) so that the air goes through the recorder at a constant speed. Do not let your breath taper off at the end so that the sound sags.

A correct sound on the recorder lasting four seconds might be drawn like this:

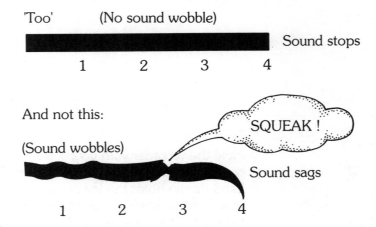

'Too'   (No sound wobble)

Sound stops

1   2   3   4

And not this:

(Sound wobbles)

SQUEAK !

Sound sags

1   2   3   4

Try to end a long sound by suddenly stopping your breath. Short notes can be stopped by bringing the tongue to the teeth.

To make your sound better, practise playing long notes of about ten seconds each, trying to make the tone fuller and bigger by *gently* pushing a little more air through the recorder. But remember not to overblow or to squeak.

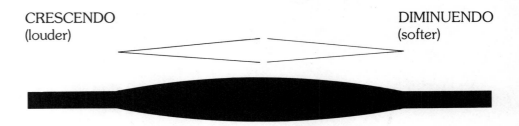

CRESCENDO
(louder)

DIMINUENDO
(softer)

When you are playing a row of notes or a flowing tune, try not to have gaps between the sounds. Do not breathe or stop between notes. A row of correctly played five B's might look like this:

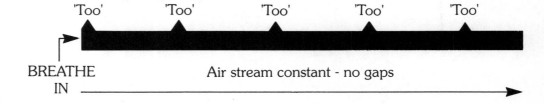

'Too'   'Too'   'Too'   'Too'   'Too'

BREATHE
IN

Air stream constant - no gaps

Always take very good care of your recorder. Never let anyone else play it. Be careful not to drop it or knock it hard on anything. After playing always dry out the inside with a small piece of cloth. Clean the instrument with disinfectant sometimes - especially the mouthpiece.

The stave

The five lines and four spaces on which music is written is called the STAVE.
Each line and space has its own letter name.

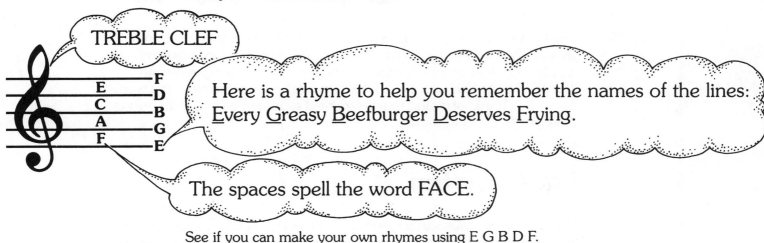

TREBLE CLEF

Here is a rhyme to help you remember the names of the lines:
Every Greasy Beefburger Deserves Frying.

The spaces spell the word FACE.

See if you can make your own rhymes using E G B D F.

Pulse and rhythm

The TIME SIGNATURE $\frac{4}{4}$ means each bar must add up to four beats.

Your heartbeat is like a musical pulse. It beats constantly (at rest) at the same
rate. In music you can imitate your heartbeat with a row of crotchets
(quarter notes):

Bar lines split up the notes into groups of four crotchets.

A CROTCHET lasts for ONE beat.

A MINIM (or HALF NOTE)
lasts for TWO beats.

Clap the following rhythm duet with a friend:

Listening skills (1)

There's no better way to start a music lesson than to play some listening games. They help you to listen very carefully and are a good starting point for improvisation, in jazz or other styles. You can play the games with your teacher or/and with other pupils, in large or small groups. You won't use written music of course, but the printed examples below might help to show you how to get started.

I got rhythm

The first player plays a short rhythm on one note and the second player (or group) repeats it. If you play in a group, each player in turn can make up a new rhythm while the others listen and repeat it.

Question and answer

The first player plays a short rhythm on one note and the second player answers with a different rhythm. In a group lesson, simply play in turn.

Name that rhythm

The first player starts, playing the rhythm of a well known tune. The others have to guess the name and join in if possible.

Can you name this tune?

■ More listening skills on page 12.

The note B

The note A

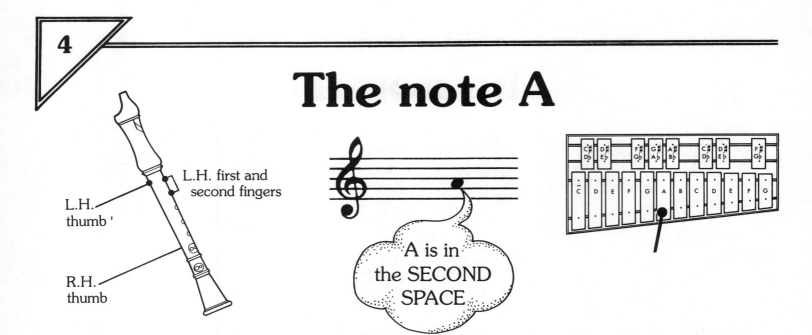

L.H. first and second fingers

L.H. thumb

R.H. thumb

A is in the SECOND SPACE

One and two note tunes

Police siren

London chimes

Slowly

Accompaniment

Pavane

Accompaniment

* Percussion symbols used in this book

 Triangle   Drum or Tabor   Tambourine

 Maracas   Cymbal

The note G

Two and three-note tunes

Of mice and men

■ Pupils unable to read the rhythm accurately should beat the pulse.

■ Performance suggestion: all pupils play throughout - twice through in groups - recorder duet only - percussion only - final play through for all.

Accompaniment

■ Ensemble parts for treble recorder, B♭, F and E♭ instruments as well as bass clef instruments, are provided in the supplement.

Merrily we roll along

Brightly

Traditional

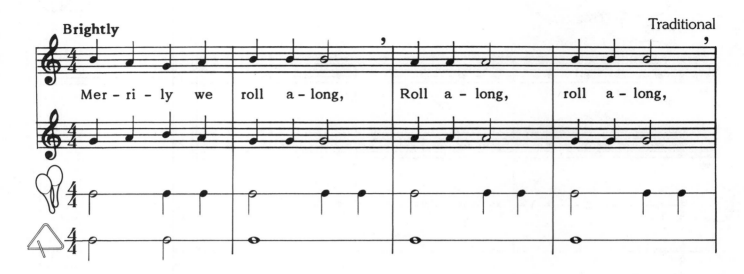

Mer – ri – ly we roll a – long, Roll a – long, roll a – long,

Mer – ri – ly we roll a – long All the live – long day.

Accompaniment

■ Children who require more practice with G, A,B should use the material in Appendix 1, page 40.
Pupils unable to read the rhythm of the percussion part should beat the pulse.

More three-note tunes

B, A and G together

Suo gan

Traditional

Slowly

Peter played with one hammer

Traditional

Brightly

The bells of St. Martin's

Round

Stately

(1)   (2)

Acapulco Bay

Tempo di Beguine

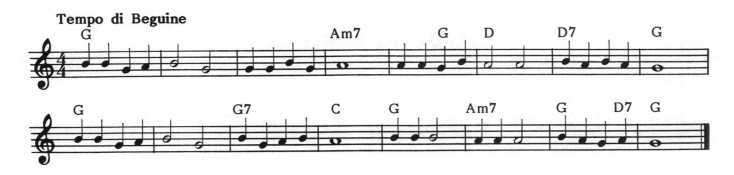

The note C

L.H second finger

L.H. thumb

R.H. thumb

C is in the THIRD SPACE

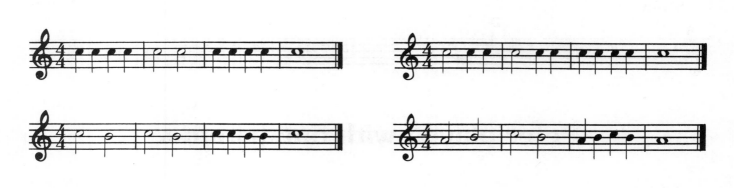

Pease pudding hot

Traditional

Fast

Flowing

Slowly

Around the sea

Moderately

(1)   (2)   (3)   (4)

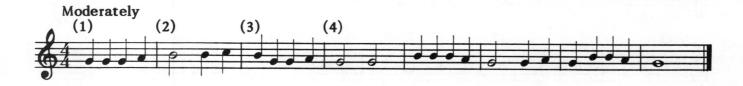

Au clair de la lune

■ When there is no piano accompaniment available play only to letter A

Whole bar (or SEMIBREVE) rest

■ *Au clair de la lune* is intended primarily as an instrumental piece but children might turn it into a song for a festival such as harvest for example. The following words might be helpful in making a start:
Now the summer's ending, crops are gathered in....

Listening skills (2)

The listening games on page 2 were all based on the note B. The new ones (below) start with the notes G, A & B. As you gain confidence, C & D can also be used, but it is important not to make up anything too complicated to begin with. Remember to keep all your phrases short and simple.

Action replay

The first player plays a short tune on, say, three notes and the second player or group repeats it. In a group, each player in turn can make up a new tune while the others listen and repeat it.

Hands off

The first player makes up a short tune using three or four notes and the next player has to answer it with a different tune. In a group, each player in turn can make up a new tune.

The first pupil plays the beginning of the well-known tune. The other players have to guess the name of the tune and try to complete it.

Upper D

thumb hole open

L.H. second finger

R.H thumb

Upper D has the FOURTH LINE going through it.

The CD player!

Leap about

Step round

The two dots mean that the music should be REPEATED.

Welsh tune

Lightly row

Now the day is over

S. BARING-GOULD
(1834 - 1924)

Slowly

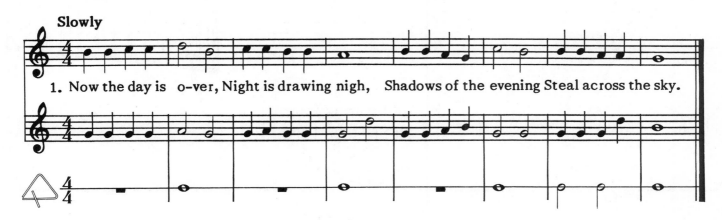

1. Now the day is o-ver, Night is drawing nigh, Shadows of the evening Steal across the sky.

Accompaniment

2. Now the darkness gathers,
Stars begin to peep,
Birds and beasts and flowers,
Soon will be asleep.

3. When the morning wakens,
Then may I arise,
Pure, and fresh, and sinless,
In thy holy eyes.

■ Now the day is over is ideal for a late afternoon assembly, an evening service, or indeed as a class prayer immediately before dismissal at the end of the day.

Jazzily

Continue

Low D

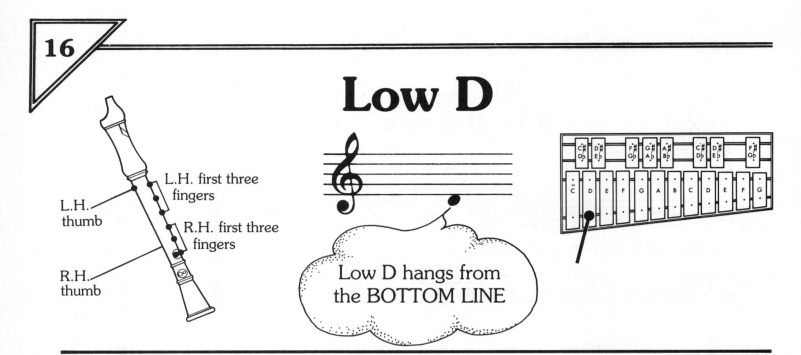

L.H. thumb

L.H. first three fingers

R.H. first three fingers

R.H. thumb

Low D hangs from the BOTTOM LINE

Cover up

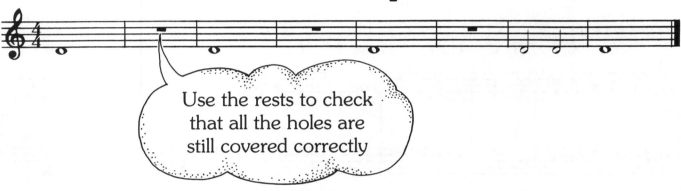

Use the rests to check that all the holes are still covered correctly

D high jump

Round Bagdad

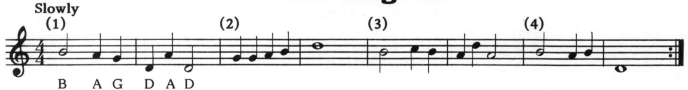

Slowly
(1)　　　　　　　　(2)　　　　　　　(3)　　　　　　(4)

B　　A　G　　D　A　D

B	C	G	A
B	A	G	D
A	B	A	D
D	A	D	A
D	B	A	B

Round Bagdad is based on the letter names of G,A,B,C & D. Find more three-letter words in the wordsearch and see if you can make up your own tune based on them. Copy your work onto manuscript paper, and write the note names underneath.

When the corn is planted

Traditional

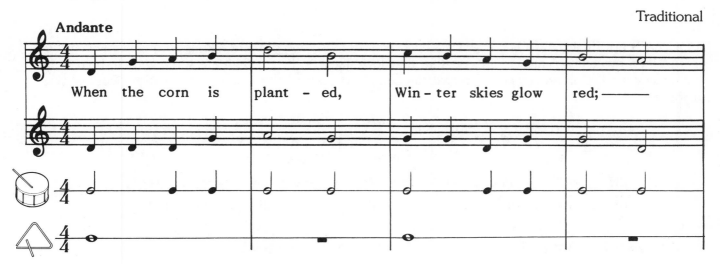

When the corn is plant - ed, Win - ter skies glow red;——

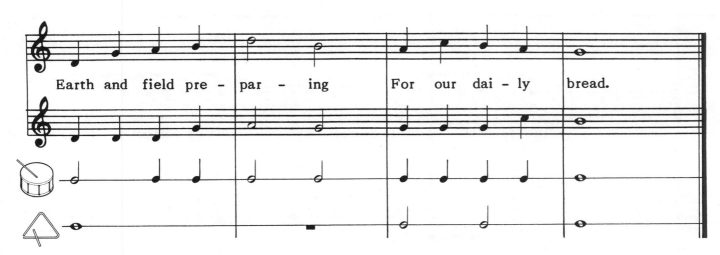

Earth and field pre - par - ing For our dai - ly bread.

Accompaniment

2. God sends sun and showers,
   Birds sing overhead,
   While the corn is growing
   For our daily bread.

3. When the corn is gathered,
   Stored in barn and shed,
   Then we all are thankful
   For our daily bread.

Moderately

Continue

Quavers

A QUAVER (or EIGHTH NOTE) ♪ is a half - beat note, so two of them add up to one whole crotchet beat. When two quavers are written together they look like this ♫. Here are some ways to help you understand the difference between crotchet beats and quaver beats. If you see a rhythm like this, you might say :

	1	2 and 3	4 and	1 and 2 and 3	4
or:	walk	run-ning walk	run-ning	run-ning run-ning walk	(rest)
or:	da	di-di da	di-di	di-di di-di da	(rest)

In the pieces below always talk and clap through the rhythms before you play.

p (soft)　(getting louder)　mf (half-loud)　f (loud)　(getting softer)　p (soft)

p piano　crescendo　mf mezzo-forte　f forte　diminuendo　p piano

Trumpet round

Brightly

I want someone to buy me a pony

Traditional

Trotting along

Supplement

Supplementary parts for wind, brass and strings

International Music Publications Limited

Of mice and men
(Moderately)

Treble recorder part

B♭ part

E♭ part

F part

Bass clef part

Merrily we roll along
(Brightly)

Traditional

Treble recorder part

B♭ part

E♭ part

8

F part

Bass clef part

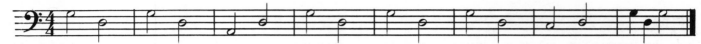

11

Au clair de la lune
(Not fast)

Traditional

Treble recorder part

Bb part

Eb part

F part

Bass clef part

Now the day is over
(Slowly)

Treble recorder part

B♭ part

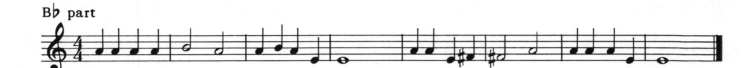

E♭ part

F part

Bass clef part

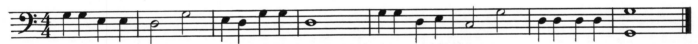

When the corn is planted
(Andante)

Treble recorder part

B♭ part

17

Eb part

F part

Bass clef part

25

Good King Wenceslas
(Fast)

Traditional

Treble recorder part

Bb part

Eb part

F part

Bass clef part

Ode to joy

(Allegro)

LUDWIG VAN BEETHOVEN
(1770 - 1827)

Treble recorder part

Bb part

New world symphony

(Andante)

ANTONIN DVOŘÁK
(1841 - 1904)

Michael row the boat ashore
(Flowing)

Traditional

35

F part

Bass clef part

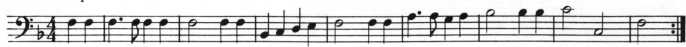

36

Kum ba ya

Traditional

Treble recorder part

B♭ part

E♭ part

F part

Bass clef part

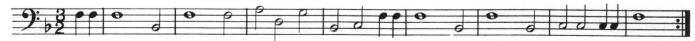

Shepherds' hey

Traditional

Low E

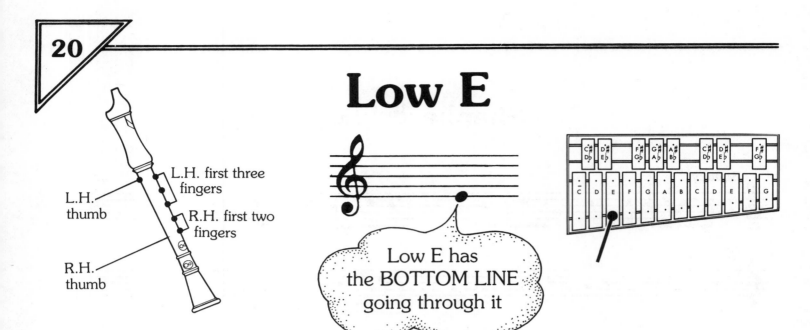

Low E has the BOTTOM LINE going through it

L.H. thumb

L.H. first three fingers

R.H. first two fingers

R.H. thumb

Sad leaps

Old Macdonald had some fries!

Sprightly

Traditional

Bad egg round

Slowly

(1)   (2)   (3)   (4)

B   A   D   E   G   G

Slurs

When two or more notes are joined with a slur, only the first note is tongued. The other notes are played smoothly (legato) without a break in the sound (in the same breath).

too-oo-oo   too-oo-oo   too - oo - oo   etc.

Sharks

Menacingly

Slur round

Slowly
(1)   (2)   (3)   (4)

Yo, heave ho

Traditional

Ploddingly

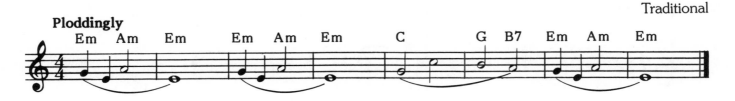

■ Some of the pieces earlier in the book can be slurred all the way through: *Suo gan* (p.9), *D high jump* (p.16) *When the corn is planted* (p.17) & *Sad leaps* (p.20).

End-a-tune

Finishing off a tune 'by ear' is not too difficult when it's well-known, but ending a tune you don't know can be more tricky. But here's how you do it! First play the beginning of the tune a couple of times, trying to 'sing along' in your mind. Then play it again, and where the written music ends, hum or whistle your ending. Then try to play it on your recorder. Remember there are no right or wrong answers - a tune might end in several different ways.

Look at the following:

Which ending do you like the best? Can you make up a better ending of your own? Why do you think all the tunes end on G? (Now try finishing off the melodies below.)
When you are happy with an ending, write the finished tune on manuscript paper. Always use pencil, so any mistakes can be corrected easily.

Make sure each bar adds up to four beats.

The note F♯

24

Love me tender

Words and Music by
VERA MATSON &
ELVIS PRESLEY

Agadoo

Words and Music by
M.SYMILE, M.DELANCERY
& J.PERAM

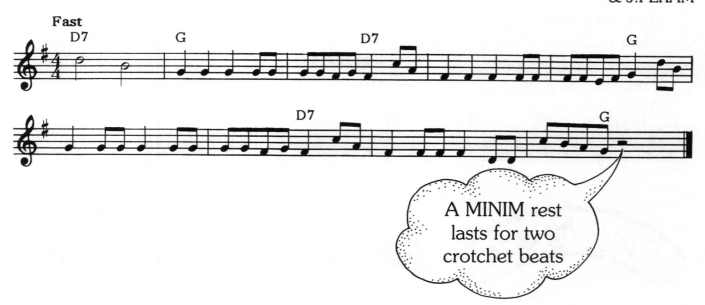

A MINIM rest
lasts for two
crotchet beats

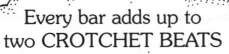

Accompaniment

The dotted crotchet

A dot after a note increases it's beat value by a half. So a dotted crotchet lasts for one and a half beats.

Play this row of crotchets and quavers:

Now join the crotchets and quavers 'in your head' and play the rhythm again, Saying *ah* into the recorder instead of *ta*. Finally, play the rhythm in the dotted crotchet/quaver form:

DOTTED CROTCHET

Deck the halls

Brightly

Traditional

Jingle bells

Festively

Traditional

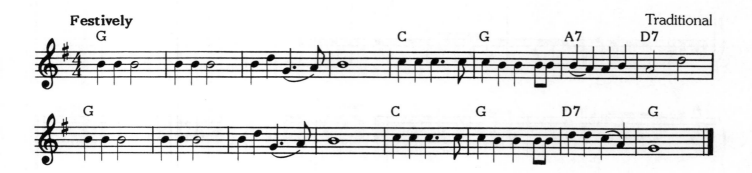

Ode to joy

LUDWIG VAN
BEETHOVEN
(1770 - 1827)

Accompaniment

Upper E

Hole left half open (pinched)

L.H. first three fingers

R.H. first and second fingers

R.H. thumb

Upper E is in the TOP SPACE

Pinching the back hole

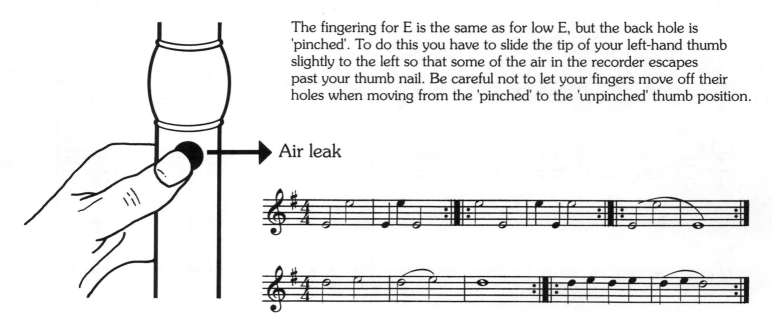

The fingering for E is the same as for low E, but the back hole is 'pinched'. To do this you have to slide the tip of your left-hand thumb slightly to the left so that some of the air in the recorder escapes past your thumb nail. Be careful not to let your fingers move off their holes when moving from the 'pinched' to the 'unpinched' thumb position.

Air leak

This old man

Traditional

Brightly

play by ear

Slowly

Continue

Auld lang syne

Traditional

Auld lang syne is based on the five notes G, A, B, D & E. The low, two - note chord played on the keyboard in the first part of the song is called a DRONE, and this is what gives the piece it's 'bagpipe effect'. Make up your own melody using the notes above. Here are three beginnings for you:

The Loch Ness monster   The lone piper   The Highland fling

New world symphony

ANTONIN DVOŘÁK
(1841 - 1904)

Frère Jacques

$\frac{3}{4}$ Time

In $\frac{3}{4}$ time every bar adds up to THREE CROTCHET BEATS

1 2 3 1 2 3 1 2 3 & 1 2 3 1 2 & 3 & 1 2 & 3 1 & 2 & 3 & 1 2 3

Count as above ; or use French rhythm names ; or use word rhythms - 'walk, running' etc.

Round lullaby

Soothingly and slow

Morning
EDVARD GRIEG (1843 - 1907)

Brightly

Roundabout

Andante

More melodies up to E

Eriskay love lilt

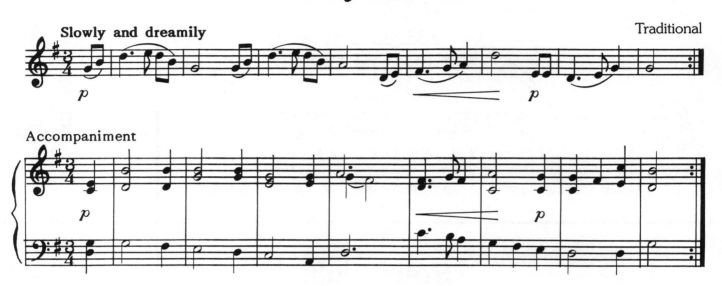

God save the Queen

Don't sit under the apple tree

Words and Music by
LEW BROWN,
CHARLIE TOBIAS,
& SAM H STEPT

The line joining these notes is called a TIE.
Play only the FIRST note, but
hold the sound for both.

Away in a manger

W.J.KIRKPATRICK
(1838 - 1921)

Westminster chimes

There's a hole in my bucket

Traditional

The note F

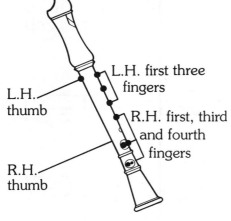

L.H. first three fingers

L.H. thumb

R.H. first, third and fourth fingers

R.H. thumb

F is in the FIRST SPACE

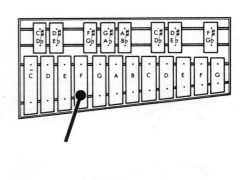

Au clair de la lune

Moderately · **Traditional**

Sad round

Slowly
(1)   (2)   (3)   (4)

Little brown jug

Jumpily · **Traditional**

Play by ear

Sprightly

Continue

The note B♭

The FLAT lowers the pitch of a note by ONE SEMITONE.

B♭ has the MIDDLE LINE going through it.

The FLAT on the middle line makes all the B's flat

The key signature of F major

Michael row the boat ashore

Flowing

Traditional

mf

Accompaniment

mf

Kum ba ya

Not fast

Traditional

f

Accompaniment

f

■ More music using F & B♭ on pages 41 & 42.

Upper F

L.H. thumb

Hole left half open (pinched)

R.H. thumb

L.H. first three fingers

R.H. first and third fingers

Upper F has the TOP LINE going through it

Scale and arpeggio of F

Slowly

Feeling the pinch

Slowly (tongued and slurred)

Play by ear

Trotting along

Continue

How much is that doggie in the window?

Words and Music by
BOB MERRILL

Lilting

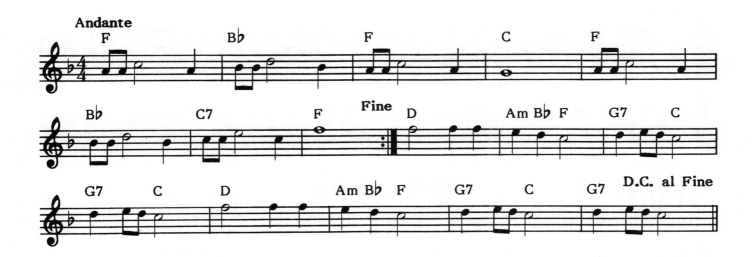

Little donkey

Words and Music by
ERIC BOSWELL

Andante

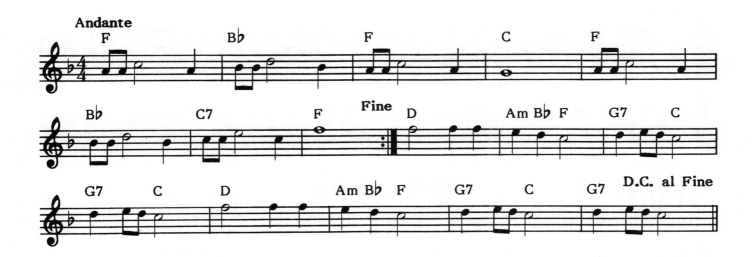

The grand old Duke of York

March   Traditional

Appendix 1

(Easy descant ensemble)

Now the day is over

(page 15 in TEAM RECORDER)

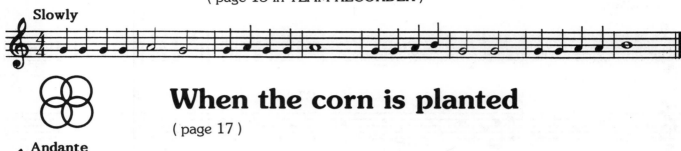

When the corn is planted

(page 17)

Good King Wenceslas

(page 25)

Ode to joy

(page 27)

New world symphony

(page 30)

Appendix 2

(Descant ensemble with TEAM BRASS/WOODWIND/PERCUSSION)

German Tune

(page 14 in all TEAM BRASS/WOODWIND/PERCUSSION BOOKS)

Blowin' in the wind
(page 20)

Words and Music by
BOB DYLAN

When I first came to this land
(page 20)

Au clair de la lune
(page 37)

Little donkey
(page 37)